The CRUNCH

Recent economic conditions require a new definition of a number of financial and business terms. This tongue in cheek dictionary explains both the original term and a new alternative meaning for modern times.

An essential humorous read for anyone involved or interested in the world of commerce, finance, industry and investment.

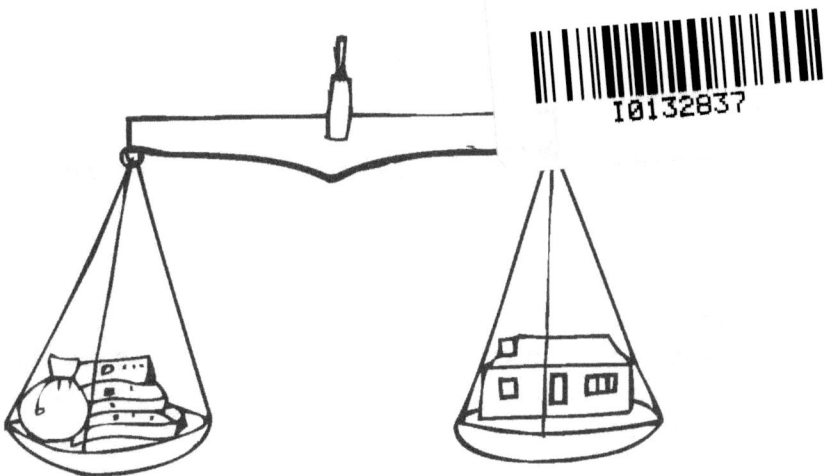

www.skillsfx.net

For more books, information and personal development training materials

A

Accident insurance
A financial product which, in return for a regular payment, protects policyholders against the financial impact of having an injury and the need to take time off work to recover

Alternative meaning
*An insurance policy that pays out if you accidentally damage your dentures (acci**dent**)*

Across the board
A movement or trend in the stock market that affects almost all stocks in all sectors, to move in the same direction

Alternative meaning
An action that is in contradiction to a previously agreed executive decision (this action goes across the board)

Accrual basis
An accounting practice where expenses and income are accounted for as if they are earned or incurred, whether or not they have been received or paid

Alternative meaning
A term for when lots of problems build daily on top of each other (these problems occur on a cruel basis)

Aftermarket
The market in which securities are traded after they are initially offered in the primary market

Alternative meaning
The place where unemployed financial services personnel search for best value food products (food is often found after the market shuts)

The Alternative Investment Market (AIM)
AIM is the London Stock Exchange's international market for smaller growing companies

Alternative meaning
Absolutely Impossible Market – The investment area where stocks and shares are impossible to predict (similar to the FTSE)

Air passenger duty
Air passenger duty is a departure tax levied on most air travel

Alternative meaning
The requirements on passengers to tackle terrorists trying to get into the flight cabin (come on let's go, it is our passenger duty)

Annual general meeting (AGM)
A meeting of shareholders held once a year at which the managers of a company report on the year's results

Alternative meaning
Aggravated Gloomy Mass – The name given to angry shareholders attending the annual company shareholder meeting

Amortisation
The repayment of a loan by instalments

Alternative meaning
When the feeling of love for a particular market or investment strategy market has reduced

Analyst
Employee of a brokerage or fund management house who studies companies and makes buy and sell recommendations

Alternative meaning
The body part most affected after stocks drop more than 5%

Annual rate of return
The rate of return you receive on an annual basis from an investment

Alternative meaning
The number of people annually who put money back under the bed rather than investing in stocks and shares

Annual Percentage Rate (APR)
The true cost of borrowing including all fees and charges

Alternative meaning
The Annualised Pressure Rate is the average blood pressure rate over a year as a result of interest rates charged during that period

Appreciation
Increase in the value of an asset

Alternative meaning
The phone call you make to a fund manager following notification that there is money left in your fund after expenses, fees and losses

Arm's length price
The price at which a willing buyer and a willing unrelated seller freely agree to transact

Alternative meaning
The name given to an asset as it becomes so embarrassingly worthless that you have to keep it at arms length

Asset
Any possession that has value

Alternative meaning
Anything that causes you considerable pain in this area

Assignment
The process of transferring property from one person to another

Alternative meaning
A sign or notice placed anywhere in a building asking for employment opportunities (A sign meant to attract job offers)

At par
A price equal to the nominal or face value of a security

Alternative meaning
A expression that is used when all else fails and notification is given that the rest of the day will be spent at the golf club

Audit trail
Resolves the validity of an accounting entry by providing a step-by-step record by which the information and data can be traced to its source

Alternative meaning
A common phrase used for the route taken by auditors following their disappearance from a company

Additional Voluntary Contributions (AVC)
Additional money paid into something in order to secure additional benefits from those contributions

Alternative meaning
Assisting volatile Companies – The act of paying a proportion of hard earned cash (often tax) into companies to bail them out

Average
An arithmetic mean return of selected stocks

Alternative meaning
An investment strategy that for many is unattainable and one that a high proportion of fund managers can only dream of achieving

Average daily balance
A method for calculating interest in which the balance owed each day by a customer is divided by the number of days

Alternative meaning
The average time that an employee within financial services is able to stand up unaided

B

Baby bond
A bond with a maturity or face value of less than a certain amount

Alternative meaning
An investment that will grow to be a pain for the next twenty years and ends up costing you more and more

Back Office
The clerical operations that support the front end of the business

Alternative meaning
The place where you now sleep and live during the week

Back dating
A feature allowing fund holders to use an earlier date on a letter of intent to invest in a mutual fund, in exchange for a reduced sales charge

Alternative meaning
When everything is lost, this is often something that you have to get involved in again (I am back dating, as my spouse has left me)

Back-end loan fund
A mutual fund that charges investors a fee to sell (redeem) shares

Alternative meaning
An investment that's very unattractive (looks like the back-end of a bus)

Back-to-back financing
An intercompany loan channelled through a bank

Alternative meaning
When two or more people make an investment decision because their backs are against the wall

Back up

When bond yields rise and prices fall, the market is said to backup. When one security is swapped into another of shorter current maturity

Alternative meaning

That moment when stocks rise again after a fall

Bad delivery

The tender and receipt process in which the necessary paperwork is not in order for some reason

Alternative meaning

Something you wish you had never posted. Often used to describe an unwise investment application completed and then posted

Bailing out

In the context of securities, refers to selling a security or commodity quickly regardless of the price

Alternative meaning

That moment when board members leave their executive plane in order to escape investigation

Bailout bond

A bond issued by the Resolution Funding Corporation to save the failing savings and loan associations in the late 1980s and early 1990s

Alternative meaning

The money one personally has spare in order to secure release from jail

Balance sheet exposure

An accounting loss that does not directly affect income statement (profit and loss account) and cash flow statement

Alternative meaning

When executive expenses for saunas and lap dancing clubs is exposed

Balance sheet identity
Where total assets equal total liabilities plus total stockholders' equity

Alternative meaning
The moment when the person responsible for everything is identified

Balance of payments
An accounting record of all transactions made by a country over a certain time period

Alternative meaning
The anticipated time you might be able to pay back the rest of the money that you owe to people (I can pay the balance of the payment...)

Balance transfer
A credit card that allows new customers to transfer an existing outstanding balance from an old card to a new one

Alternative meaning
The act of leaning heavily on a colleague because you are unable to stand on your own two feet

Balloon interest
The interest paid on a loan with large payment at maturity

Alternative meaning
The number of people who have expressed an interest in, or are leaving the finance industry by air (often a hot air balloon under the radar)

Balloon maturity
A repayment schedule for an issue of bonds in which a large number of the bonds come due at the same time, typically the final maturity date

Alternative meaning
The name given to the money required in order to pay for the retirement party for an employee (Can we afford balloons at the maturity party?)

Bank
An institution providing a wide range of day-to-day services for your financial needs

Alternative meaning
Something that you cannot bank on in times of financial turmoil or need

Bank collection float
The time that elapses between when a cheque is deposited into a bank account and when the funds are available to the depositor

Alternative meaning
The number of customers who have jumped ship in the last day

Bank draft
A draft addressed to a bank

Alternative meaning
The name given to the current state of repair of a bank building due to lack of reinvestment and cold winds

Bank wire
A computer messaging system linking major banks

Alternative meaning
The security measures used to keep cash hungry customers away from the premises during a cash crisis (often means barbed wire)

Bankmail
A bank's agreement with a company attempting a takeover not to finance any other potential acquirer's bid

Alternative meaning
The illegal act of one bank blackmailing another

Bankruptcy
The inability to pay ones debts

Alternative meaning
When a bank implodes on itself (comes from the word eruption)

Barrier options
Option contracts with trigger points that, when crossed, automatically generate the buying or selling of other options

Alternative meaning
The options that one country has to both attack and defend its financial and economic security from that of another country (used in Iceland)

Bear market
Any market in which prices exhibit a declining trend for a prolonged period of time (usually falling by 20% or more)

Alternative meaning
The name given to an investment market where investors are no longer able to cope or bare the losses made

Bear spread
A strategy in the options market designed to take advantage of a fall in the price of a security or commodity, usually executed by buying a combination of buys and sells on the same security at different strike prices in order to profit as the security's price falls

Alternative meaning
The cheapest type of meat spread available in the supermarket

Beating the gun
Gaining advantage through a quick response to market developments

Alternative meaning
The act where a group of traders play Russian roulette

Benchmark
The performance of predetermined securities for comparison purposes

Alternative meaning
The marks made by teeth or nails during day-to-day stock trading

BETA
The measure of a fund's or a stock's risk in relation to the market or to an alternative benchmark. A beta of 1.5 means that a stock's excess return is expected to move 1.5 times the market excess returns

Alternative meaning
The number of times you have lost money or have been beaten by the market that day (I was beat again)

Bid
The price a potential buyer is willing to pay for a security

Alternative meaning
The act of placing an investment fund on eBay with no reserve price in the hope that you will receive bids for it

Billing cycle
Elapsed time between billing periods for goods sold or services given

Alternative meaning
The projected costs associated by replacing company cars with bicycles or other self powered transportation

Black Friday
A quick drop in a financial market - The original Black Friday occurred on 24th September 1869 as prospectors tried to corner the gold market

Alternative meaning
The last day of the week

Block list
In the context of general equities it is the listing of stock an investment bank is wants to buy or wants to sell at the beginning of the day

Alternative meaning
A list of clients that you just do not want to take a call from

Blue chip
A large, prestigious, prosperous and stable corporation

Alternative meaning
An investment that leaves you feeling depressed, blue and with a chip on your shoulder

Bond
A written and signed promise to pay a certain sum of money on a certain date, or on fulfilment of a specified condition

Alternative meaning
Something that you buy into and then are unable to honour (your word is not your bond in this case)

Bond swap
The sale of one bond issue and purchase of another simultaneously

Alternative meaning
When the value of a total fund is worth less that the complete DVD set of 007, James Bond movies

Book value
A company's total assets minus intangible assets and liabilities

Alternative meaning
When the value of the paper proving investment ownership is worth more than the assets that these reflect

Branch
An operation in a foreign country incorporated in the home country

Alternative meaning
Part of an organisation that can snap very easily

Break-even point
Refers to the price at which a transaction produces neither a gain or loss

Alternative meaning
The level of frustration reached when the lead in a pencil has completely worn down due to stress (common at board meetings)

Breakup value
The break-up market value of all divisions of a company, if they were each independent and established their own market stock prices

Alternative meaning
Where the value of the total impending divorce settlements of the fund's investors is worth more than the actual fund itself

Broker
A person who acts as an intermediary between a buyer and seller, usually charging a commission

Alternative meaning
Where you go if things need fixing (another name for psychologist - I'm going to see my broker)

Budget
A detailed schedule of financial activity for a given period, such as an advertising budget, sales budget, or a capital budget

Alternative meaning
The amount required to be spent on marketing and promotion in order to get rid of something unwanted (it is impossible to budge it)

Building society
A financial organisation that is owned by its members not shareholders

Alternative meaning
An area of the country where all land is being built on (including green belt and conservation areas)

Bull
An investor who thinks that the market will rise

Alternative meaning
The amount of hype surrounding a particular investment

Buy to let mortgage
A loan secured against a property, where the borrower intends the property to be rented to tenants rather than used as their own residence

Alternative meaning
A mortgage where the borrower buys a property and lets other people pay for it (buy to let other people pay for it)

C

Cash against documents (CAD)
A transaction in which the buyer assumes the title for the goods being purchased upon paying the sale price in cash

Alternative meaning
When a friend fails to pay back money they owe you (they are a cad)

Call risk
The combination of cash flow uncertainty and reinvestment risk introduced by a call provision

Alternative meaning
The percentage chance during the day of receiving a call from an unhappy investor or client

CAP
An upper limit on the interest rate on a loan

Alternative meaning
The money you need to survive. Buskers found that they received more money if they placed a larger cap on the ground, up to a certain limit

Capital asset
A long term asset such as land or a building that is not purchased or sold in the normal course of business

Alternative meaning
The percentage ownership a government has in key companies, such as banks and utilities (The capital has assets of…...)

Capital budgeting
Determining which potential long-term projects are worth undertaking

Alternative meaning
Staying four in a room when away on business trips

Capital gain
When a stock is sold for a profit, the capital gain is the difference between the net sales price and the original purchase price

Alternative meaning
The amount of profit a government is likely to make in the future, from purchasing failing companies using taxpayer money

Capital gains tax
The tax levied on profits from the sale of capital assets

Alternative meaning
The tax that residents of a capital city pay to the government for the increase in their property values during the year

Capital rationing
Placing limits on the amount of new investment undertaken by a firm, either by using a higher cost of capital, or by setting a maximum budget

Alternative meaning
The need to reduce public services in an area, due to poor financial management (originates from the rationing needed during the war)

Capitalisation
The sum of a corporation's long-term debt, stock and retained earnings

Alternative meaning
Making something seem profitable by using capital letters

Carrot equity
Slang for an equity investment with the added benefit of an opportunity to purchase more equity if the company reaches certain financial goals

Alternative meaning
The value of an allotment of shares or the retail sales value of the fruit and vegetables grown in your garden

Carrying charge
The fee a broker charges for carrying securities on credit

Alternative meaning
The fee paid by ex employees to remove their boxes from the office

Cash and carry
Options strategy in which a futures contract is sold and a matching cash contract is bought to profit from their price discrepancy

Alternative meaning
The most popular place to purchase food for corporate entertainment

Cash cow
A company that pays out most of its earnings per share to shareholders as dividends or generates a steady and significant amount of cash flow

Alternative meaning
The process of assessing liquidity within an agricultural fund

Cash on delivery (COD)
In the context of securities, this refers to the practice of institutional investors paying the full purchase price for securities in cash

Alternative meaning
The act of investing cash in Iceland for greater returns

Cash plus convertible
A convertible bond that requires cash payment upon conversion

Alternative meaning
The money received from the sale of a soft top, cabriolet or convertible company car

Cash surrender value
The amount an insurance company will pay if the policyholder cashes in a whole life insurance policy

Alternative meaning
The ransom one is likely to receive for the kidnap of key financial personnel within an organisation

Ceiling
The highest price, interest rate, or other numerical factor allowable in a financial transaction

Alternative meaning
The stress level indicators of those working on the trading floor

Certified cheque
A bank guaranteed cheque for which the funds are immediately withdrawn, and for which the bank is legally liable

Alternative meaning
A cheque that only a totally crazy person would be prepared to sign (they signed it – they should be certified)

Chastity bonds
Bonds redeemable at par value in the case of a takeover

Alternative meaning
Investments that lock you out for a considerable period of time during which you are unable to access your money in any way

Chinese wall
A communication barrier between financiers at a firm and traders to prevent the sharing of inside information that bankers are likely to have

Alternative meaning
A point or level in the Asian market that stocks cannot seem to get over

Chip and pin
Technology where consumers type in a four digit personal identification number rather than sign their name when paying for goods

Alternative meaning
When a shareholder interrupts a shareholder meeting and pins the CEO up against the wall demanding answers (they chip in and pin up)

Clean up
The purchase or sale of all the remaining supply of stock, or the last piece of a block in a trade leaving a net zero position

Alternative meaning
The cost of cleaning the stock exchange after a day of heavy trading

Close a position
To eliminate an investment from one's portfolio, by either selling a long position or covering a short position

Alternative meaning
To shut all bank tills before worried customer's rush to withdraw cash

Collection
Process of recovering amounts owed to a firm by its customers

Alternative meaning
The act of asking for hand outs and favours from colleagues in the office, prior to your final day

Comfort letter
An informal letter from a bank indicating its willingness to support a customer with a short term loan, if and when required

Alternative meaning
A letter from a certified psychiatric specialist confirming that you were of unsound mind at the time of making a certain investment decision

Common shares
Shares that usually entitle the shareholders to vote at shareholder meetings and receive profit through dividends

Alternative meaning
Shares that a lot of people own and therefore should not be discussed when attending high society events (these shares are so common)

Conglomerate
A firm engaged in two or more unrelated businesses

Alternative meaning
A sticky corporate mess

Constructive receipt
The date a taxpayer receives dividends or other income

Alternative meaning
Official written acknowledgement that one is to be sacked or fired

Consumer interest
Interest paid on consumer loans, credit cards and retail purchases

Alternative meaning
The level of interest that consumers have in government policies and decisions (historically very low)

Convertibility
The ability to exchange a currency without government restrictions or controls

Alternative meaning
The process of getting something of little value changed into something of no value

Cooling off period
The time period in which a customer can change their mind about certain types of contracts and purchases

Alternative meaning
The time taken for the heart beat to return to normal after seeing a statement of investment value

Core competence
A primary area of expertise or narrowly defined fields or tasks at which a company or individual excels

Alternative meaning
The look of sheer surprise referred to when the right decision is made by someone in authority (cor competence at last)

Counter trade
The exchange of goods for other goods rather than for cash

Alternative meaning
The act of infiltrating another and stealing information bank by letting a member of your bank teller staff seek employment with them

Coupon
The periodic interest payment made to bond holders during its life

Alternative meaning
Vouchers given to staff instead of bonuses or other remuneration

Covenant
Provisions in an agreement that require certain specified actions to either take place (affirmative) or be refrained from (negative)

Alternative meaning
Investments that include witchcraft and black magic (from coven)

Covered call
The selling of a call option while simultaneously holding an equivalent position in the underlying stock in an attempt to take advantage of a neutral or declining stock

Alternative meaning
The process of encouraging traders to trade outside the building, under a temporary roof in order to save office rent, heat and electricity

Credit
A contractual agreement in which a borrower receives something of value now and agrees to repay the lender at some later date

Alternative meaning
That which is nearly impossible to obtain

Current account
An account with a financial institution used for day to day personal banking purposes

Alternative meaning
A new form of account for saving towards the ever increasing cost of electricity prices

Cushion Bonds
High income bonds that sell at only at a moderate premium because they are callable at a price below that at which a comparable non-callable bond would sell

Alternative meaning
Bonds that perform so poorly the fund managers and investors can sleep during the normal trading day (this is so boring, get a cushion)

'This little piggy went to market and this little piggy went home'

D

Daily price limit
The level or a limit at which many commodity, futures, and options markets are allowed to rise or fall in a day

Alternative meaning
The maximum amount an investor is prepared to lose during a day

Date of record
Date on which holders of record in a firm's stock ledger are designated as the recipients of either dividends or stock rights

Alternative meaning
The initial date that a financial expert is charged with malpractice

Deal stock
Stock subject to merger or acquisition, either publicly or rumoured

Alternative meaning
Stock that has a risk rating similar to roulette or black jack

Debenture
A promissory note or a corporate bond which (in the US) is backed generally only by the reputation and integrity of the borrower and (in the UK) by the borrower's specific assets

Alternative meaning
An investment that has no teeth and is under performing

Default
Failure to make timely payment of interest or principal on a debt security or to otherwise fail to comply with the provisions of a loan

Alternative meaning
A French term used to blame a specific individual for poor investment performance (it is 'the fault' of the fund manager)

Deferred call
A provision that prohibits a company from calling the bond before a certain date and during this period the bond is said to be call protected

Alternative meaning
The third call that you have made to your psychologist today

Deflation
Decline in the prices of goods and services and the opposite of inflation

Alternative meaning
The personal feeling you have when your investments are falling

Delayed opening
Postponement of the start of trading in a stock until the correction of a gross imbalance in buy and sell orders occurs

Alternative meaning
Postponement of trading because things are bad or the act of opening your investment statement later because you know it contains bad news

Delisting
Removal of a company's security from listing on an exchange because the firm has not abided by specific regulations

Alternative meaning
The movement of a share from the A list (top performer) to the D list (the fund value is in the negative)

Denomination
Corresponds to the face value of currency units, coins, and securities

Alternative meaning
The name of the religious sector that a failed stockbroker chooses after redundancy or resignation

Deposit
Funds placed into an account or a down payment given in advance to support or help guarantee the intention to complete the transaction

Alternative meaning
Securing a mortgage by guaranteeing to deposit the future potential earnings of your children with the institution lending the money

Depression
The time period when there is a drop in economic activity resulting in mass unemployment, over supply against demand, falling or reducing prices, lack of confidence and many other factors

Alternative meaning
The name given to the mark the hands make on the face when the head is in them for the second hour of that day (from impression)

Director
An individual who carries out certain tasks within a company in accordance with the regulations, charter or articles of that company

Alternative meaning
Someone who points out the direction that they want other people to take but do not intend to take themselves

Discount
A deduction from something in some form

Alternative meaning
The amount you are prepared to give away to get rid of something

Disposable income
Gross income less direct taxes or what you have left in your hand

Alternative meaning
Income that you used to have but it has now been trashed or binned

Dividend
A portion of a companies profit paid out to shareholders

Alternative meaning
An income you used to receive but because it has been shared between so many people it is now worthless (from divide)

Double bottom
A term used in technical analysis to refer to the drop of a stock's price, a rebound, and then a drop back to the same level as the original drop

Alternative meaning
When something of value reduces by twice what it should have done, in half the time that it should have taken, with twice the impact

Downturn
A negative change in the economy

Alternative meaning
The actions taken by people during financial hardship when they turn down their heating (also used when people turn down the hems of skirts and also trouser legs to stay warm and save money on new clothes)

Draft
A rough version of a document prior to it being reviewed and finalised

Alternative meaning
The amount of wind entering a building due to less money being spent on office maintenance and repair (a higher draft increases sickness and absence rates though so is counter-productive)

Due diligence
The internal audit of a target firm by the acquiring firm

Alternative meaning
Diligence that was due but arrived too late

E

Each way
A broker's commission for their involvement in the purchase and sale

Alternative meaning
The condition where market falls occur in all directions and there is no way out (I look each way and trouble is coming)

Earn out
Business valuation formula that relates the final purchase price of a firm to its future earnings

Alternative meaning
The fees and bonuses that senior executives earn out of a crumbling organisation before they leave (I can earn an extra xxxx out of this)

Earnings retention ratio
The amount of money a company retains for reinvestment purposes

Alternative meaning
The amount of money available for second homes, golf fees, luxury goods, bonuses and other vital things

Elephants
A term used to refer to large institutional investors

Alternative meaning
Investors who will never forget what has happened to them

Embedded option
An option that is part of the structure of a bond that gives either the bondholder or the issuer the right to take some action against the other

Alternative meaning
When staying in bed is the only option

Emergency fund

A reserve of cash kept available to meet the costs of any unexpected financial emergencies

Alternative meaning

The amount of money retained within an organisation to enable it to continue to pay executive bonuses following financial difficulties

Enterprise

A business or firm engaged in business activities

Alternative meaning

A business that decides to begin operations in an unknown territory (from a famous science fiction series)

Equity

The ownership or interest in a business or the residual value of an asset

Alternative meaning

The union that executives join, so that they can act in the way they act

Equity kicker

Loan agreement under which a lender agrees to charge lower than normal interest rates in return for a share of ownership in the property or business for which loan is advanced

Alternative meaning

A politician who negatively influences equities through their words and actions (common during the 2008 credit crisis)

Euro

The name for the composite monetary unit that has replaced national currencies in several European countries

Alternative meaning

A slang term used when someone owes you money (You're owed €20)

Ex-dividend date
The first day of trading when the seller, rather than the buyer, of a stock will be entitled to the most recently announced dividend payment

Alternative meaning
The last date you are likely to receive an income from your ex spouse

Exercise
To implement your right as the holder of an option to buy or sell

Alternative meaning
The physical activity associated with trying to find out where your money has been invested

Exhaust price
The low price at which a broker must liquidate a client's holding in a stock purchased in a margin account in order to meet a margin call

Alternative meaning
The final price one will accept for an investment after all other options have been explored (we've exhausted all options)

Expiration date
The last day (in the case of American style) or the only day (in the case of European style) on which an option may be exercised

Alternative meaning
The lifetime expectancy of an individual working in the stock market

External funds
Funds coming into a company from an outside source in order to increase cash flow and aid expansion plans

Alternative meaning
The funds held in offshore or tax efficient jurisdictions for use by key people at some later stage (often used for retirement or incentives)

Extraordinary call
Early redemption of a revenue bond because the revenue source paying the interest on the bond has been eliminated or has disappeared

Alternative meaning
A call from your advisor to tell you that your investment is doing well

F

Face value

For a debt security this is the amount that an issuer agrees to pay at the maturity date. For an equity security, face value is usually a very small amount that usually bears no relationship to its market price

Alternative meaning

The amount your broker says your investment is worth when meeting you face to face (often less than the real value)

Fall out of bed

A sudden drop in a stock's price resulting from failed or business deals that have gone bad or fallen through

Alternative meaning

The consequence of looking at stock values whilst sitting in bed

Financial engineering

Combining or carving up existing financial products to create new ones

Alternative meaning

The process of surrounding simple financial products with jargon and definitions, that might, or might not, at any time now, or in the future, be or not be confusing!

Financial leverage

The degree to which an investor or business uses borrowed money

Alternative meaning

Borrowing so much money that you tip yourself into financial turmoil

Financial pyramid

A structure to spread risk across low, medium and high risk vehicles

Alternative meaning

The name given when initial investors support those at the top

Finder's fee
A fee a person or company charges for service as an intermediary

Alternative meaning
The money paid to investigators to try and find out where your profit has disappeared too

Five Cs of credit
Five characteristics often used to form a judgment about a customer's creditworthiness: character, capacity, capital, collateral, and conditions

Alternative meaning
The 5 consequences of taking up all the credit offers that you receive through the post (chaos, confusion, crisis, collapse, concern)

Fixation
The process of setting the present or future price of a commodity

Alternative meaning
An obsessive concern with an investment over a long period of time

Flag
A technical analysis term referring to a chart pattern created when a steep rise (or fall) is followed by trading in a narrow price range, followed by a steep rise (or fall)

Alternative meaning
The feeling of lack of energy or enthusiasm following a day at work

Flat
A market with little movement or trading

Alternative meaning
The only type of accommodation people are able to afford following the maturity of their pension plans

Flip side
In the context of general equities it is the opposite side to a proposition or position (to buy if sell is the proposition and vice versa)

Alternative meaning
When the only alternative or option is to work in a burger bar

Floater
A fixed income instrument which has a coupon rate or interest rate that varies based on a short term rate index

Alternative meaning
An investment that you cannot get rid of no matter what you do to it

Floor
The area of a stock exchange where active trading occurs or the price at which a stop order is activated

Alternative meaning
A temporary sleeping location for a night or two, or week, or month

Floor trader
An exchange member who trades on the floor for their own account

Alternative meaning
An ex trader who now makes a living selling carpets or tiles

Flurry
A drastic volume increase in a specific security

Alternative meaning
A meal eaten when you cannot afford a curry

Footsie
Popular name for the FTSE 100

Alternative meaning
The act of gambling with the market under the table

Forced conversion
Occurs when a convertible security is called in by the issuer, usually when the underlying stock is selling well above the conversion price

Alternative meaning
The need to add more bedrooms to ones property in order to afford mortgage payments (I was forced to convert my house)

Forex
The currency of another country

Alternative meaning
A low value investment that you leave for your ex spouse

Free fall
When financial markets are falling indiscriminately

Alternative meaning
Markets tend to do this in September and October (in autumn/ fall)

Frictional cost
The cost associated with exchange of goods or services and incurred in overcoming market imperfections

Alternative meaning
The price that working in the finance industry can have on your home and family life (it causes a lot of friction)

G

Gilt

A long-term fixed income debt security (bond) issued by the UK government and traded on the London stock exchange

Alternative meaning
Something you invest in and have this feeling afterwards

Going public

When a private company first offers shares to the public market and investors

Alternative meaning
The act of a company admitting its liabilities

Going short

Selling a share, bond or commodity before actually buying it

Alternative meaning
To allow your family to eat first due to lack of food (common in 2008)

Grace period

The time period stipulated in most loan contracts and insurance policies when a late payment will not result in default or cancellation

Alternative meaning
The period of time between agreeing and signing when one prays that nothing will go wrong

Graduated security

A security that has moved from one exchange to another

Alternative meaning
A security offered by a student or novice in the market

Grandfather clause
A provision that exempts a company already conducting business in the area from being restricted or penalised by a new rule or regulation

Alternative meaning
A way of securing extra funds based upon the future earnings of your children's children

Gross earnings
A person's total taxable income prior to adjustments

Alternative meaning
The generic name given to executive salaries, incomes and bonuses

Gross estate
The total value of a person's property and assets before accounting for debts, taxes, and liabilities

Alternative meaning
A term often used for the houses, land and other assets owned by politicians and other government figures

Guarantee
The assumption of responsibility for payment of a debt or performance of some obligation, if the liable party fails to perform to expectations

Alternative meaning
Something that is guaranteed, unless something else has an impact on it

Gun jumping
In the context of securities trading it refers to trading in a security on the basis of information that has not been made available to the public

Alternative meaning
The act of gate crashing firing ranges in order to end the nightmare

H

Haircut

The margin or difference between the actual market value of a security and the value assessed by the lending side of a transaction

Alternative meaning

A process of selling ones hair to raise cash during hard financial times

Hard currency

A freely convertible currency that is not expected to depreciate in value in the foreseeable future

Alternative meaning

A currency that is difficult and hard to sell

Heavy

An equities market now dominated by sellers, or oversupply, resulting in falling prices

Alternative meaning

The general term given to the feeling one has when an executive lunch costing shareholders £500 per head, has been eaten

Hedge fund

A fund that employs a variety of techniques to enhance returns, such as both buying and shorting stocks, according to a valuation model

Alternative meaning

A fund where the value of its assets are worth less than the gardens and plants of the investors within the fund

High flyer

A high priced, highly speculative stock that has moved up rapidly

Alternative meaning

When a group of executives on a business trip meet onboard

Hold

A recommendation by an analyst not positive enough on a stock to recommend a buy, but not negative enough to recommend a sell

Alternative meaning

The cheapest way of flying on business travel due to corporate expenses being reduced (it can get cold in the hold though)

House account

A type of account at a brokerage firm that is given a high level of priority and is handled by the main office or an executive

Alternative meaning

An account where money is deposited to pay for upcoming household bills and expenses (requires a minimum balance of £2,000)

I

Identified shares
Stock or a mutual fund whose purchase date and price can be identified for capital gains and tax purposes to differentiate them from additional shares, normally to reduce tax

Alternative meaning
Shares where the real name of the owner can be identified

Inactive asset
An asset not used in a productive manner at all times

Alternative meaning
The situation where human intelligence is not used when making an investment decision (the brain is inactive)

Incentive fee
An incentive paid to anyone managing funds who achieves above average returns and performance

Alternative meaning
Financial remuneration paid in order for a certain course of action to be taken or not taken by someone who may or may not be known

Income tax
An annual tax imposed on an individual's net profit

Alternative meaning
Money a government receives to fund the salaries, expenses and other needs of government employees, friends, family and acquaintances

Indemnify
To compensate someone for loss or damage

Alternative meaning
A get out of jail free card

Inflation
The rate at which the general level of prices for goods and services is increasing

Alternative meaning
The act of pumping prices up so that more profit can be made by companies, their executives and the shares they own in these businesses

Inside market
The highest bid and lowest offer price by market makers for their own inventories

Alternative meaning
Renting a market stall to sell company goods and possessions cheaply for personal gain (pens, paper, whitener, coffee, tea, magazines etc)

Insolvent
A firm that is unable to pay debts (liabilities exceed assets)

Alternative meaning
The act of glue sniffing due to long term redundancy and depression

Interest only mortgages
A loan for the purchase of a home where the payment of principal is deferred and interest payments are the only current obligation

Alternative meaning
Mortgages that many people show an interest in but are unable to afford

Interim dividend
The declaration and payment of a dividend prior to annual earnings being calculated

Alternative meaning
Something given in order to keep people quiet for a period of time

Internal expansion
Growth of assets due to internal financing or appreciation

Alternative meaning
The amount of increase in employee jacket and trouser size due to growing salaries, bonuses and corporate entertainment

Invoice
A bill written by a seller of goods or services and submitted to a purchaser for payment

Alternative meaning
The moment of truth when a company or fund makes a statement of explanation (the board are said to be in-voice with each other)

Issue
A stock or bond is offered for sale by a corporation or government entity, usually through an underwriter or in a private placement

Alternative meaning
The problems that investors have with their investments

J

Joint bond
A bond that is guaranteed by the issuer and a party other than the issuer

Alternative meaning
An investment that specialises in drug and pharmaceutical companies

Joint return
An income tax filing status operated in some countries where a married couple's income and deductions can be combined

Alternative meaning
The situation where a couple work for the same company and they both become unemployed at the same time

Joint will
One will covering both husband and wife

Alternative meaning
When two people work together towards a common purpose or aim

Junk bond
Junk or high-yield bonds that offer investors higher yields than bonds of more financially sound companies

Alternative meaning
A bond whose average return is flat like the bottom of the Chinese boat with that same name

Justified price
The fair market price of an asset

Alternative meaning
The additional items and sundry extras added to a valuation in order to justify the price being asked for it

K

Key performance indicators (KPI)
A set of measures that help a company to determine if it is reaching its performance and operational goals

Alternative meaning
A ratio used to let company executives know how often their staff are entering and leaving the premises and offices (locking/unlocking doors)

Key person insurance
A life insurance policy purchased by a company to insure the life of a key executive. The company is the beneficiary on death

Alternative meaning
Insurance that pays out if a key person within a business does a runner and takes vital company information and documents with them

Kickback
An illegal, secret payment made in return for a referral resulting in a transaction or contract

Alternative meaning
The response of a market to artificial stimulators such as the injection of large amounts of cash

Killer bee
An investment banker who creates strategies to help a target company avoid a hostile takeover by making itself less attractive or harder to acquire

Alternative meaning
An investment contract that has a painful sting in its tail (such as a penalty charge or cancellation fee)

L

Late charge
A fee a credit grantor charges a borrower for a late payment

Alternative meaning
The upwards movement of a particular market or index during the last few hours of trading

Layup
An easily executed trade or order

Alternative meaning
The time needed to rest following stock losses

Lend
To provide money temporarily on the condition that it or its equivalent will be returned, often with an interest fee

Alternative meaning
The ancient process of loaning money in exchange for agreed repayments and interest (often difficult to come by)

Letter of intent
A letter most often issued as acknowledgment of the fact that a merger between companies or an acquisition is being considered seriously

Alternative meaning
A letter to a customer confirming that subject to a full moon, a North Easterly wind and a low tide, their request for credit may be considered

Leg
One side of an option spread that can be either long or short

Alternative meaning
The new method of moving between meetings within a city in order to save costs (let's walk, it's not far)

Liability
An obligation legally binding an individual or company to settle a debt

Alternative meaning
The money owed by an organisation. Often in direct correlation to the weaknesses of those in charge (hence the term 'he is a liability')

LIBOR
London Interbank Offered Rate

Alternative meaning
Ludicrous Interest Banks Ordinarily Request

Life annuity
An annuity that pays a fixed amount for the lifetime of the annuitant

Alternative meaning
The name given to an individual who spends their working life within the investment and finance industry

Line of credit
A loan arrangement between a bank and a customer allowing that customer to borrow up to a pre-specified amount of money

Alternative meaning
The name given to pre-purchased hard drugs (white powder)

Liquid asset
An asset that can easily and cheaply be converted into cash

Alternative meaning
An alternative name for alcohol

Liquidation
The process of disposing of assets within a failed company with the proceeds used to pay creditors. Any remaining money can then be distributed to shareholders

Alternative meaning
An event where a great deal of alcohol is consumed in order to drown out the day's sorrows

Load
The sales fee charged to an investor when shares are purchased in a load fund or annuity

Alternative meaning
The stress associated with a type of investment

Long bonds
Bonds with a long current maturity

Alternative meaning
An investment vehicle you have to keep for a long time in order to make a return on it

Long run
A period of time, longer than one year, in which all costs are variable

Alternative meaning
The physical activity taken following the negative valuation of your investment portfolio

Loss leader
A product or service sold at a substantial discount in order to generate additional sales

Alternative meaning
A CEO who destroys the profitability of a company

M

Maintenance call
A call for additional money or securities when a margin account falls below its exchange mandated required level

Alternative meaning
A call to ones ex spouse to discuss financial arrangements

Margin
Using money borrowed from a broker/dealer to purchase securities

Alternative meaning
The area on a piece of make where the most important information is often written (frequently used for personal notes, views and opinions)

Margin call
A demand for additional funds because of adverse price movement

Alternative meaning
The process of saving money by purchasing paper with no margins

Market cycle
The period between the two latest highs or lows of the S&P 500, showing net performance of a fund through an up and a down market

Alternative meaning
The name for what used to be called the pool car (now a bicycle)

Market jitters
When a particular financial market becomes nervous about the current situation and often responds wildly to the smallest changes in sentiment

Alternative meaning
An investment condition where ones needs to visit the toilet on a frequent basis

Market overhang
Anxiety among many investors, causing them to sell stocks and bonds, pushing prices down

Alternative meaning
The size of the stomach protruding over the waistline due to excessive business entertaining

Market sweep
An offering following a tender offer, allowing institutional investors to obtain a controlling interest at a price higher than the original offer

Alternative meaning
The individual who clears rubbish from the trading floor

Maturity
The date on which a debt becomes due for payment

Alternative meaning
The age reached when a senior manager considers all information prior to making important decisions (they have reached maturity)

Maturity value
The amount that an issuer agrees to pay at the maturity date

Alternative meaning
The value placed on a trader when they reach the age of fifty. As a result of their experience and wisdom

Mob spread
The yield spread between a tax-free municipal bond and a treasury bond with the same maturity

Alternative meaning
The average age of unhappy and protesting investors

Mock trading
The simulated trading of securities used as a learning device for training investors and brokers

Alternative meaning
This is the unpleasant act of laughing and playing practical jokes on junior traders

Mortality tables
Data compiled by insurance companies on the rate of death among groups of people categorised according to age or other factors

Alternative meaning
A table consisting of details of the institutions and funds that are about to die away or become non existent

Mortgage pool
A group of mortgages with similar class, interest rate, and maturity characteristics

Alternative meaning
A loan secured against the value of the water within a swimming pool

Mutual fund
A pool of money managed by an investment company that offers investors a variety of goals, depending on the fund type

Alternative meaning
A fund where everybody benefits from it, it if performs

Mystery shopper
A person hired by a market research firm or a manufacturer to visit retail stores, posing as a casual shopper to collect information

Alternative meaning
That hard to get customer during a recession

N

Naked option
An uncovered option for which the buyer or seller does not own the underlying asset

Alternative meaning
The process of exploring all future career options by looking at the stripping, lap dancing and adult film industries

Near money
Non cash but liquid assets that can be easily converted into cash but are not used as a medium of exchange in everyday transactions

Alternative meaning
Money in your pocket or within a one metre range (real money)

Net income
Income after tax and other mandatory deductions

Alternative meaning
The income generated from shipping, fishing and marine funds

Net worth
The company's total earnings, reflecting adjustments for the cost of doing business, depreciation, interest, taxes and other expenses

Alternative meaning
An indication of personal wealth and prosperity linked to the ability to afford fresh salmon

New issue
Securities publicly offered for the first time, whether in an IPO or as an additional issue of stocks or bonds by a company already public

Alternative meaning
Another thing that is likely to go totally wrong

No book
A situation that arises when there is little or no interest in buying or selling a particular security

Alternative meaning
When all assets within an office are sold, including all books

Non compete
A provision in an employment contracts that prohibits an employee from working for a competing firm for a specified number of years after the employee leaves the firm

Alternative meaning
The act of placing oneself in a loosing position

Non purpose loan
A loan with securities pledged as collateral, but which is not to be used in securities trading or transactions

Alternative meaning
A loan that is taken for the purpose of living on a day-to-day basis

Notice day
In futures markets this is the day on which notices of intent to deliver actual commodities against a contract (not cancelled out by matching orders) are given

Alternative meaning
The day that a Government realises that they need to take action

Notification date
The day the option is either exercised or expires

Alternative meaning
The day something of immense consequence is communicated (this day is often quite a while after the original event became known)

Null and void
No longer valid or enforceable

Alternative meaning
The personal feeling you may have when you discover that your pension pot is worthless and completely empty

O

Obligation bond

A mortgage bond with a face value greater than the value of the underlying property, designed to compensate the lender for any costs that might exceed the value of the mortgage

Alternative meaning

An agreement that has to be followed through by an individual who marries the son or daughter of an investment banker

Odd lot

A trading order for less than 100 shares of stock

Alternative meaning

Investors who invest in unusual or strange areas

Off floor order

An order a customer places with a broker not on the floor of an exchange and has a preference over on floor orders

Alternative meaning

An offer than causes the purchaser to suffer extreme stress and collapse after investing (please help me get up off the floor)

Offer

The lowest price that any investor or dealer has declared that he/she will sell a given security or commodity for

Alternative meaning

The panic state of asking for any offer to sell something

Offering date

The date on which an offering will first be available to the public

Alternative meaning

Letting it be known that you are single again

Offerings
Often refers to initial public offerings. When a firm goes public and makes an offering of stock to the market

Alternative meaning
Sandwiches, sweets, cakes and other perishable goods left for staff following board meetings. Normally free

Offset
Elimination of a long or short position by making an opposite transaction

Alternative meaning
What happens that nobody else sees (taken from the film industry)

On the print
To participate in a block trade that has already transpired, as if that customer had been part of the trade originally. Often used by a new party looking to participate in a trade that has just happened

Alternative meaning
When the only option for a Government is to print more money and release it into the system. The term can also be used for counterfeiting and is considered an alternative strategy to re-capitalisation

On the run
The most recently issued government bond in a maturity range

Alternative meaning
The action senior executives take following business collapse

One-man picture
When both bid and the offered prices come from the same source

Alternative meaning
When only one employee photograph is left on the company family tree

Open account
An arrangement whereby sales are made with no formal debt contract

Alternative meaning
An account that any hacker can access

Operating cycle
The average time between the acquisition of materials or services and the final cash realisation from that acquisition

Alternative meaning
The costs associated with maintaining all company bicycles

Operating profit
Revenue from a firm's regular activities less costs and expenses, and before income deductions

Alternative meaning
The money received from the sale of ones blood, hair and organs

Option
Gives the buyer the right, but not the obligation, to buy or sell an asset at a set price on or before a given date

Alternative meaning
Another name for hope

Oral contract
A contract not recorded on paper or on computer but made vocally. It is normally legally enforceable

Alternative meaning
An agreement to model your teeth in order to bring in extra income during times of financial hardship

Original face value
The principal amount of a mortgage or investment at its issue date

Alternative meaning
The value you were originally informed about during a face to face meeting (often less than the real value)

Overdraft
Provision of instant credit by a lending institution

Alternative meaning
The cost of heating and staff sickness due to lack of windows and doors in an uncompleted building

Overhead
The ongoing administrative expenses of a business which cannot be attributed to any specific business activity, but are still necessary for the business to function

Alternative meaning
The generic name given for the problems you are currently experiencing within your job (I have this overhead and it's worrying)

Over issue
An excess of issued shares over authorised shares

Alternative meaning
A really big problem

Overnight position
A broker dealer's position in a security at the end of a trading day

Alternative meaning
How comfortably one is able to sleep based upon the business climate for that day (my overnight position was uncomfortable, I am aching)

P

Package mortgage
A mortgage on a house and the property within the house

Alternative meaning
A loan given to an individual to purchase a flat pack house that they then build themselves

Paid up
When all payments that are due have been made

Alternative meaning
The name given to the staff lottery that is no longer in operation due to lack of contributions and interest

Paper gain or loss
An unrealised capital gain or loss based on a comparison of current market price to original cost

Alternative meaning
Any gain or loss made by acting on the advice of financial news editors

Par
The nominal or face value printed on a security

Alternative meaning
The act of leaving work early to play golf

Par value
The value of a loan stock that will be paid when it is redeemed

Alternative meaning
The ability of employees to be able to pay for annual golf club membership (I have a fifty percent par value this year – can pay half)

Participating fees
The portion of total fees in a syndicated credit that go to the participating banks

Alternative meaning
The cost required to be involved in a decision about ones own future

Pass-through
A security representing pooled debt obligations that pass income from debtors to its shareholders

Alternative meaning
The rate at which people become unemployed within a business (we have a pass-through rate of twenty percent)

Pass the book
The process of transferring responsibility for a brokerage firm's trading account from one office to another around the world in order to benefit from trading 24 hours a day

Alternative meaning
A book where bets are taken on the probability of an individual still being employed in a certain period of defined time (will Bob be here in 7 days time – four to one)

Path-dependent option
An option whose value depends on the sequence of prices of the underlying asset rather than just the final price of that asset

Alternative meaning
The process of deciding what you will say as you walk up the path to your front door, after a bad day at the office

Pattern
A technical chart formation used to make market predictions by following the price movements of securities

Alternative meaning
The behaviour of looking at the wall rather than a stock index graph because the pattern on the wall is easier to understand

Pound
The currency of Britain

Alternative meaning
Investments negatively hit by market conditions (It has been pounded)

Price earnings ratio (P/E ratio)
A ratio that is equal to a stock's market capitalisation divided by its after-tax earnings over a 12-month period

Alternative meaning
The percentage chance of you having to either sell or return to wearing your old school physical education (PE) clothes, due to lack of money

Pegging
Making transactions in a security, currency, or commodity in order to stabilise or target its value through market intervention

Alternative meaning
The act of drying your clothes at work to save money (paperclips can be used instead of pegs to save even more money)

Perfect hedge
A situation in which the profit and loss from the underlying asset and the hedge position are equal

Alternative meaning
A hedge that protects the garden and its vegetables perfectly

Performance fund
A fund investing in growth and performance stock with low dividends

Alternative meaning
A fund that has such a stage presence that is a hard act to follow

Perpetual bond
A nonredeemable bond with no maturity date, that pays regular interest rates indefinitely

Alternative meaning
A bond whose performance will always come back to haunt you

Personal trust
An interest in an asset held by a trustee for the benefit of another person

Alternative meaning
The situation where you use personal guarantees and finance in order to support the business you are involved in (I have trussed a lot of my own money in this or I am trussed up)

Phone switching
Transferring money between funds in the same mutual fund family by telephone request

Alternative meaning
The act of using someone else's phone in order to save money on calls

Piggybacking
Illegal trading by a broker who trades stocks, bonds or commodities in a personal account following a trade just made for a customer

Alternative meaning
The act of returning bacon sandwiches for a full refund after less than half of them have been eaten (take the piggy back)

Pip
Used for listed equity securities, it is the smallest unit of a currency

Alternative meaning
The act of scouring bins for edible fruit that one then consumes or uses to make fruit juice

Plant
The assets of a business including land, buildings, machinery and all equipment permanently employed

Alternative meaning
Often the only living thing in the office that is prepared to listen to you

Plow back
To reinvest earnings in the business rather than pay out dividends

Alternative meaning
The act of investing bonuses and spare money into your personal development, family and future (maybe to set up a farm)

Plug
A variable that handles financial slack in a financial plan

Alternative meaning
The action of removing the plugs from old electronic goods in order to sell or use them for personal gain

Plus tick
A stock market transaction (sometimes a quote) at a price higher than the preceding one for the same security

Alternative meaning
When personal itching and irritation is above normal levels due to stress and pressure

Policy loan
A loan made, often below-market interest rate, from an insurance company to a policyholder and secured on its cash surrender value

Alternative meaning
Borrowing from the government to survive their policies and errors

Portability
The ability for certain benefits to be carried from job to job

Alternative meaning
The illegal act of removing alcohol meant for corporate entertainment purposes to your own house for personal consumption (the theft of port used to be very common and now includes all business alcohol)

Portfolio
A collection of investments, both real and financial

Alternative meaning
Nothing left an investment (from the naval term port left)

Positive carry
The difference between the cost of financing the purchase of an asset and the asset's cash yield where the cash yield is greater

Alternative meaning
To move personal possessions back into a building after notification that you are not redundant or that you have got your job back

Precious metals
Gold, silver, platinum, and palladium, which are used for their intrinsic value or for their value in production

Alternative meaning
The value of jewellery worn by employees that can be used as security for a business loan if things get really bad

Preferred stock
Stock where a dividend is paid before any dividends to common stock holders and takes precedence in the event of liquidation

Alternative meaning
The best content and value soup within the canteen

Present value
The amount of cash today that is equivalent in value to a payment, or to a stream of payments, to be received in the future

Alternative meaning
The value of gifts given to someone leaving, this reflects the economic situation at that time (in 2008 a 2 for 1 meal voucher was common)

Previous balance method
A method of calculating finance charges based on the account balance at the end of the previous month

Alternative meaning
The way one used to balance things before it was realised that it did not work and that things were getting worse (common in banks)

Price discovery process
The process of determining the prices of assets in the marketplace through the interactions of buyers and sellers

Alternative meaning
Uncovering the true cost and value of something through research and the use of private investigators

Price leadership
A price charged by a dominant producer that becomes the norm

Alternative meaning
The impact and consequences of leadership decisions, pay and bonuses

Priced out

The situation when the market has already adjusted the price of a security in light of a specific piece of news or information

Alternative meaning
When one cannot afford to eat in the places where one used to eat

Private market value (PMV)

The break-up market value of all divisions of a company if the divisions were each independent and established their own market stock prices

Alternative meaning
The real value given to things after a few drinks behind closed doors

Privatisation

The transfer of government-owned or government-run companies to the private sector, usually by selling them

Alternative meaning
The act of joining the Army following redundancy

Probability

The relative likelihood of a particular outcome among all possible outcomes available

Alternative meaning
Another name for hope

Profit

The positive gain from an investment or business operation after subtracting for all expenses

Alternative meaning
An ancient word, not used for many years (it meant consultation and praying to the Gods to secure the future)

Profit-sharing plan
An incentive system where employees share in company profits through a cash fund or a deferred plan used to buy stock or bonds

Alternative meaning
The act of employing family and friends within a business even though they may not have the skills or experience required

Projection
The use of econometric models to forecast the future performance of a company, country or other financial entity using historical and current information

Alternative meaning
The need for presenters to use personal torches and bulbs for presentations as all projectors have been sold to release capital

Proxy
Authorisation that shareholders' votes may be cast by others

Alternative meaning
A strong bond between two or more people

Public debt
Issues of debt by governments to compensate for a lack of tax revenues

Alternative meaning
The amount of money each citizen is required to pay in order to maintain institutional stability and government policies

Pullback
The downward reversal of a prolonged upward price trend

Alternative meaning
The act of covering ones eyes in disbelief with some form of clothing (normally associated with impending losses of doom)

Q

Qualified opinion
Accountant's or auditor's opinion of a financial statement for which some limitations existed, such as an inability to get certain information or a significant upcoming event which may or may not occur

Alternative meaning
When a senior government figure asks their teenage son or daughter for expert advice on a situation that they have been unable to resolve

Qualifying share
Shares of common stock that a person must hold in order to qualify as a director of the issuing corporation

Alternative meaning
The degree to which you will be responsible if things go totally wrong (for board members this is often quite low)

Qualitative analysis
An analysis of the qualities of a company that cannot be measured concretely, such as management quality or employee morale

Alternative meaning
Assessing the nutritional value and content of sandwiches during a meeting or event

Quantitative analysis
An analysis of the mathematically measurable figures of a company, such as the value of assets or projected sales

Alternative meaning
Assessing the number of sandwiches against the number of attendees at a meeting to identify the number left (this helps in personal meal planning and shopping for the week)

Quality spread
The difference between Treasury and non-Treasury securities that are identical in all respects, except for quality rating

Alternative meaning
Any business lunch that does not require payment by participants (that was a quality spread)

Quick assets
Cash and other assets which can or will be converted into cash soon

Alternative meaning
Anything that can be pawned

Quoted price
The price at which the last trade of a particular security or commodity took place

Alternative meaning
The last few words heard by a trader prior to them running away from losses in the market (I cannot believe it has dropped to .....)

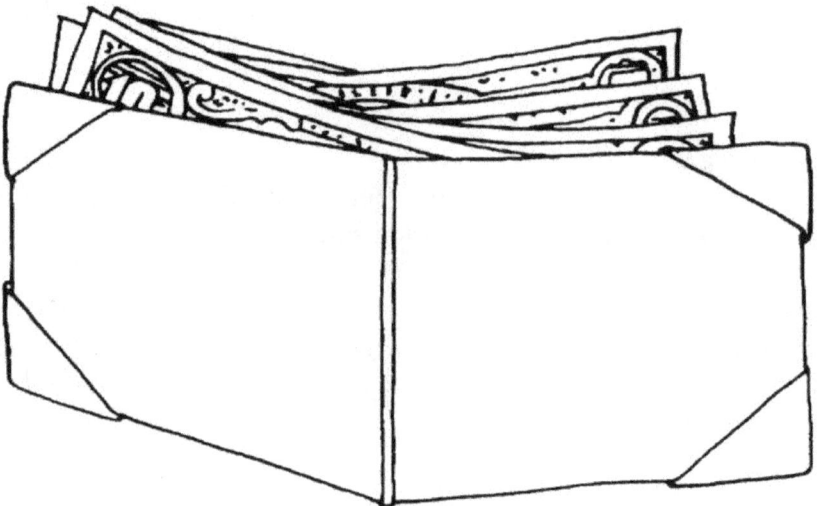

R

Radar alert
Close monitoring of trading patterns to uncover unusual buying activity that might signal a takeover attempt

Alternative meaning
The act of listening to Police channels in order to gain valuable minutes and information prior to leaving the building forever

Rally
An upward movement of prices

Alternative meaning
The formation and demonstration by a group of unhappy investors

Random variable
A function that assigns a real number to each and every possible outcome of a random experiment

Alternative meaning
Anything not previously thought of that will have an impact

Rate covenant
A covenant in certain bonds that specifies how it will be determined what rates to charge to users of the facility the bond is financing

Alternative meaning
The cost of accommodation at a local church

Real assets
Identifiable assets, such as land and buildings, equipment, patents, and trademarks, as distinguished from a financial investment

Alternative meaning
Intelligence, strength, love, care, knowledge, experience and skills

Real estate
A piece of land and whatever physical property is on it

Alternative meaning
A traditional vehicle with the ability to carry loads in the back unlike the hatchback variants of modern times

Rebate
Negotiated return of a portion of the interest earned by the lender of stock to a short seller

Alternative meaning
A debate where one goes over the same things again and again

Recession
A temporary downturn in economic activity, usually indicated by two consecutive quarters of a falling GDP

Alternative meaning
The amount your hair has receded during a week as a result of stress (I think I am due a week of heavy recession)

Recovery
A period in a business cycle following a recession where GDP rises

Alternative meaning
The anticipated time needed in a clinic or institution in order to get back to a normal physical, mental or emotional state

Redemption date
The date on which a bond matures or is redeemed

Alternative meaning
The date the devil will come back to haunt you, based on your previous decisions and actions

Red herring
From the warning printed in red, that information in the document is still being reviewed by the securities exchange commission and is subject to change

Alternative meaning
Food that has become too expensive to afford in normal day-to-day eating (today is a red herring day – a good meal is expected)

Reference rate
A benchmark interest rate (such as LIBOR) used to specify conditions of an interest rate swap or an interest rate agreement

Alternative meaning
The number of reference requests received by personnel each day

Regular way settlement
The standard basis by which some security trades are settled

Alternative meaning
An agreement with a neighbour where one crosses their property without any compensation needed

Rejection
Refusal by a financial institution to grant credit usually because of the financial history or refusal to accept the security presented

Alternative meaning
The pain of taking cash from people (the opposite of injection)

Relative strength
Stock price movement over the past year, compared to a market index

Alternative meaning
The strength and health levels of parents and relatives prior to them being sent to work to bring in extra income

Relative value
The attractiveness measured in terms of risk, liquidity and return of one instrument relative to another

Alternative meaning
The assets and future income available from parents and relatives

Residential assets
Assets that remain after sufficient assets are dedicated to meet all senior debt holders' claims in full

Alternative meaning
The value of all assets held by residents within a building which can be used as security to remortgage that building

Resident risk
The risk that is unique to a company such as a strike, the outcome of unfavourable litigation or a natural catastrophe

Alternative meaning
A secret government scale indicating the percentage chance of unrest within an area or community

Residuals
What is remaining, such as the residual value of a car after three years, which might be fifty percent

Alternative meaning
What is left within an organisation after it has been taken over

Retention rate
Retained earnings divided by total after tax earnings as a percentage

Alternative meaning
The rate at which those in charge are able to remember the mistakes they previously made and therefore not repeat them (often low)

Reverse leverage
Occurs when the interest on borrowings exceeds the return on investment of the funds that were borrowed

Alternative meaning
The act of backing your car into the office and filling the boot with office stationery to sell later for extra income

Rights offering
Issuance to shareholders that allows them to purchase additional shares, usually at a discount to market price

Alternative meaning
When one or more of the senior executives are offered as scapegoats

Rising bottoms
A chart pattern showing an increasing trend in the daily low prices of a security or commodity

Alternative meaning
The number of people leaving the office at any moment in time

Risk factor
Measurable characteristic or element, a change in which can affect the value of an asset, such as exchange rate, interest rate, and market price

Alternative meaning
A TV show where government officials take stakes in companies and then try to keep them stable for one month (no winners yet)

Riskless rate
The rate earned on a riskless investment

Alternative meaning
The percentage of the population who are not prepared to risk their money by investing in bank deposits

Risk lover
A person willing to accept higher expected rates of return on the understanding that higher amounts of risk are associated with this

Alternative meaning
A person willing to have relationships with others for personal gain

Risk management
The process of identifying and evaluating risks and selecting and managing techniques to adapt to risk exposures

Alternative meaning
The act of putting non-qualified people into senior management positions without the appropriate risk management strategies in place

Risky asset
An asset whose future return is uncertain

Alternative meaning
Any part of the body that causes an individual to loose focus and make unwise decisions

Rollover
The reinvestment of income from a business back into the business, or of the principal and interest accruing from one mature investment into a new investment

Alternative meaning
To say yes in order to keep ones job or position

Round lot
A trading order typically of 100 shares of a stock or a multiple of 100

Alternative meaning
A derogatory word for the board

Rundown

A summary of the amount and prices of a serial bond issue that is still available for purchase

Alternative meaning

The requirement for a company to save electricity costs by turning off power to the lifts (we have to run down the stairs)

S

Safe harbour

A way of reducing the likelihood of getting taken over by a target company acquiring a business so heavily regulated that it makes the target less attractive, giving it a safe harbour

Alternative meaning
An exit strategy for those leaving a country by sea

Safety cushion

An amount of leeway built into a business plan or assets available if anticipated projections are under to a certain degree

Alternative meaning
Trampolines and other soft material used to prevent injury of those jumping from buildings in suicide attempts

Scalp
To trade for small gains

Alternative meaning
The act of blaming someone else

Second round
Stage of venture capital financing following the start-up and first round

Alternative meaning
The behaviour associated with employees who go to the toilet or leave early when a second round of drinks needs to be ordered

Sector
Used to characterise a group of securities that are similar with respect to maturity, type, rating, industry or coupon

Alternative meaning
An unknown area where assets seem to vanish in a mysterious way

Seed money
Money used for the initial investment in a project or start-up company, for proof-of-concept, market research, or initial product development

Alternative meaning
Money set aside for growing home vegetables to save on food costs

Sell the book
An order by an institutional investor to sell as much of its current position as possible in a given security at the current market price

Alternative meaning
The act of selling all materials possible within an organisation in order for it to survive

Seller climax
A sudden drop in security prices as sellers dump their holdings

Alternative meaning
The moment of no return when a few seconds of joy are followed by many years of pain and suffering

Set aside
Court's action that annuls, cancels, or voids a contract, judgment, or order

Alternative meaning
To get passed over for promotion

Share
Certificates or book entries representing ownership in a corporation or similar entity

Alternative meaning
An investment you make in order to receive a share of the profits and then you keep this share yourself

Short
The state of having sold a stock short without having covered it or an individual who is holding a short in a particular security

Alternative meaning
An investment that leaves your pocket empty

Short covering
The purchase of securities by a short seller to replace those borrowed at the time of a short sale

Alternative meaning
When people have to buy small umbrellas, not large enough to fully cover or protect them from the rain, because they have little money

Short interest
Total number of shares of a security that investors have sold short and that have not been repurchased to close out the short position

Alternative meaning
Attention span during a falling market

Short sale
Borrowing a security (or commodity futures contract) from a broker and selling it, with the understanding that it must later be bought back (hopefully at a lower price) and returned to the broker

Alternative meaning
The act of selling ones old school uniform for financial gain

Short tender
Using borrowed stock to respond to a tender offer. Illegal

Alternative meaning
The amount of quality time that you can spend with your partner at the end of the day (a short tender moment)

Show and tell list
The stock an investment bank is looking for based on the requirements of actual customers

Alternative meaning
A list detailing what is really happening within a company. Normally held in a very secure area

Side by side trading
Trading a security and an option on that security, on the same exchange

Alternative meaning
Investments made with your partner

Signature loan
A good faith loan that is unsecured and requires only the borrower's signature on the loan application

Alternative meaning
The main type of loan that an institution offers and one actively promoted and marketed to potential customers (like George in ASDA)

Simple prospect
An investment opportunity in which only two outcomes are possible

Alternative meaning
A potential investor (a prospect) who has more money than sense

Single option
A single put option or call option, as opposed to a spread or straddle, which involves multiple puts and calls

Alternative meaning
An investment between partners where there is an option to split the investment if the relationship fails

Skewed distribution
Probability distribution in which an unequal number of observations lie below (negative skew) or above (positive skew) the average

Alternative meaning
A term used at a company BBQ event where the more senior members of the company get the better quality food from the grill

Skimming
A method of credit card fraud, whereby a fraudster 'skims' or reads and copies the information on the magnetic strip of a credit card

Alternative meaning
A low cost pastime popular with ex fund managers who live near the coast (flat pebbles are used to skim the water)

Skip day settlement
Settling a trade one business day beyond what is normal

Alternative meaning
The negotiation between an employer and employee that enables the employee to take an agreed day off sick

Slump
A fall in performance describing consistently falling security prices for several weeks or months

Alternative meaning
The body position of someone who has recently lost money or their job

Sour bond
A bond issue that has defaulted on interest or principal payments and will thus trade at a large discount and a poor credit rating

Alternative meaning
An investment that leaves a bad taste in your mouth

Speculation
Purchasing risky investments that present the possibility of large profits but also pose a higher than average possibility of loss

Alternative meaning
Investing in investments where the small print is so small that it is difficult to understand what one is actually investing in

Spreadsheet
A computer program that organises numerical data into rows and columns in order to calculate and make adjustments based on new data

Alternative meaning
The mess left after eating breakfast or another meal in bed

Stagnation
A period of slow economic growth, or, in securities trading, a period of inactive trading

Alternative meaning
A situation when no male member can afford to get married within a company and hence no stag nights are organised

Stakeholders
All parties that have an interest, financial or otherwise, in a project or company

Alternative meaning
Groups of shareholders with wooden stakes in their hands who are out to get the blood sucking financial vampires who took their money

Stamp duty
The tax paid on disposal of a property

Alternative meaning
The extra cost added by an office manager for sending letters internally

Stand alone principle

Investment approach that advocates a firm should accept or reject a project by comparing it with securities in the same risk class

Alternative meaning

The feeling you have when everyone else has left you

Standard deviation

The square root of the variance, which is a measure of dispersion of a set of data from its mean

Alternative meaning

The level of perverse behaviour expected within an organisation based on the normal average and what is going on at work

Standby agreement

In a rights issue, it is an agreement that the underwriter will purchase any stock not purchased by investors

Alternative meaning

How people within a company support and help each other

Standby fee

The amount paid to an underwriter who agrees to purchase any stock that is not purchased by public investors in a rights offering

Alternative meaning

The amount one has to pay for support from ones colleagues (this is often a non financial fee)

Statement of condition

A document describing the status of assets, liabilities and equities of a person or business at a particular time

Alternative meaning

A letter from your doctor or specialist

State pension
The state pension is a government run pension based on the number of 'qualifying years' someone has accumulated over a period of time

Alternative meaning
A retirement income that leaves you in a state of poverty, desperation or both (you have paid for this and therefore are entitled to it)

Stock market
A market for trading equities

Alternative meaning
A slang word for either the canteen or the market if flat (stock being a broth made from meat, fish, bones and vegetables by simmering)

Stock rating
An evaluation by a rating agency of the expected financial performance or inherent risk of common stocks

Alternative meaning
The average feedback received from those eating in the canteen

Stock ticker
A letter designation assigned to securities and mutual funds that trade on U.S. financial exchanges

Alternative meaning
The link between stock value and heartbeat (the ticker is playing up)

Stopped out
A purchase or sale that is executed under a stop order at the stop price specified by the customer

Alternative meaning
An all night corporate event

Straight line depreciation
Apportioning an equal amount of depreciation in each accounting period

Alternative meaning
When stock prices go down in a 90 degree vertical direction

Strike price
The stated price per share for which underlying stock may be purchased (in the case of a call) or sold (in the case of a put) by the option holder upon exercise of the option contract

Alternative meaning
The price or salary levels when employees are likely to go out on strike

Stripped bond
Bond that can be subdivided into a series of zero coupon bonds

Alternative meaning
Assets that are invested in adult clubs and bars

Structured debt
Debt that has been customised for the buyer, often by incorporating unusual options and facilities

Alternative meaning
Debt that has been carefully built up and engineered in a way that protects those responsible for it

Subordinated debt
Debt over which senior debt takes priority

Alternative meaning
Debt within a company that is too frightened to come to the surface

Substitute sale
A method for hedging price risk that uses debt market instruments, such as interest rate futures, or involves selling borrowed securities as the primary assets

Alternative meaning
Selling surplus people for financial gain

Suitability rules
Policies and guidelines that brokers must use to ensure that investors have the financial means to assume the risks that they wish to take

Alternative meaning
The dress code within an organisation (suitability)

Supply side economics
A theory of economics that reductions in tax rates will stimulate investment and in turn will benefit the entire society

Alternative meaning
The sale of company stationary and other goods for personal profit at car boot sales and markets (to supply things on the side)

Sushi bond
A Eurobond issued by a Japanese corporation

Alternative meaning
A potentially fishy investment

Sweat equity
An increase in equity created by the labour of the owner

Alternative meaning
The amount of perspiration caused by an equity investment

T

Take out
A cash surplus generated by the sale of one block of securities and the purchase of another

Alternative meaning
A new and more efficient way of corporate entertainment

Take a call
The act of receiving a phone call order for a trade to be completed

Alternative meaning
Happy and willing to receive job opportunities and offers by phone

Taxable event
An event or transaction that has a tax consequence, such as the sale of an asset that is subject to capital gains taxes

Alternative meaning
Everything that you do from the moment you wake up in the morning

Tax shelter
Legal methods taxpayers can use to reduce tax liabilities

Alternative meaning
The requirement to trade down to a smaller house in order to be able to pay your annual tax bill (hopefully bigger than a bus shelter)

Tax relief
The reliefs against tax that one is entitled to and can claim

Alternative meaning
Another name for death and when inheritance tax has been paid

Term bonds
Bonds whose principal is payable at maturity

Alternative meaning
An investment fund to help pay for school clothes and books

Term insurance
Provides a death benefit only, with no build up of cash value

Alternative meaning
An insurance policy to help pay for the cost of school holidays

Terminal value
The value of a bond at maturity, typically its par value, or the value of an asset on some specified future valuation date

Alternative meaning
The process of an airport authority increasing its valuation by adding the value of lost luggage to its financial accounts

Tick indicator
A market indicator based on the number of stocks whose last trade was an uptick or a downtick

Alternative meaning
The nervousness scale of traders within a particular market (a tick being an involuntary movement)

Tight money
When a restricted money supply makes credit difficult to secure

Alternative meaning
A small quantity of money within your pocket that does not interfere with your clothing line and hence is unnoticeable (also a criminal term for the tights used to cover a face during a bank robbery)

Time deposit
An interest bearing deposit with a specific maturity

Alternative meaning
A deposit that seemed sensible at the time of making it (also applies to the credit facilities jewellers used to offer on more expensive watches)

Tip
Optional payment given in addition to a required payment, usually to express appreciation for excellent service

Alternative meaning
The place you seldom visit because you now cannot afford to throw anything away (also used to describe the spam that fund managers get)

Tracker mortgages
A loan secured against a property where the interest charged is guaranteed to maintain a set relationship with, or track a base rate

Alternative meaning
Mortgages that offer reasonable terms and therefore can take a long time to find out about or track down

Trading paper
Deposits purchased by accounts that are likely to resell them

Alternative meaning
The exchange of toilet paper for favours (often due to cost reductions)

Trading range
The difference between the high and low prices traded during a period of time

Alternative meaning
A range attended by traders to relax and revitalise (often including weapons such as tanks, bazookas, missiles and other heavy armoury)

Trust
A fiduciary relationship calling for a trustee to hold the title to assets for the benefit of the beneficiary

Alternative meaning
An ancient term that has all but disappeared

Turnaround
Securities bought and sold for settlement on the same day. Also describes a firm that has been performing poorly, but changes its financial course and improves its performance

Alternative meaning
The emotions some experience as they travel into work for the day

Two tier tax system
A taxation system that results in taxing the income going to shareholders twice

Alternative meaning
A situation where both parties in a financial or business transaction are upset and angry with the result (they both shed tears)

U

Unbundling
Separation of a multinational firm's transfers of funds into discrete flows for specific purposes

Alternative meaning
The activities involved in finding out exactly what one has invested in by unbundling all the information and advice received

Uncovered call
A short call option position in which the writer does not own shares of the underlying stock represented by the option contracts

Alternative meaning
The act of making phone calls outside (often made this way due to the sensitivity of the conversation and the need to do this in the open)

Underlying
What supports the security or instrument that parties agree to exchange in a derivative contract

Alternative meaning
When a junior corporate spokesperson does not tell a complete lie (they are not lying, they are underlying)

Underwrite
To guarantee, the issuer of securities a specified price by entering into a purchase and sale agreement

Alternative meaning
The illegal act of submitting company accounts and reports that do not reflect the real position of the company (the real situation is not written, it is underwritten)

Undigested securities
Newly issued securities that are not purchased because of lack of demand during the initial public offering

Alternative meaning
Securities that can no longer be digested due to their toxic nature

Unlisted security
A security traded in the over the counter market that is not listed on an organised exchange

Alternative meaning
Assets executives own that nobody knows about

Unloading
Selling securities or commodities whose prices are dropping to minimise loss

Alternative meaning
Meetings held between shareholders in order to share and discuss their unhappiness and concerns (unloading their feelings and frustrations)

Upgrading
Raising the quality rating of a security because of new optimism about the prospects of a firm, due to tangible or intangible factors

Alternative meaning
The exchange of company cash for better seats (this often applies to airlines, trains, stadiums and theatres)

Upswing
An upward turn in a security's price after a period of falling prices

Alternative meaning
The relationship between improved golf performance and reduced business performance due to time on the golf course

Useful life

The expected period of time during which a depreciating asset will be productive

Alternative meaning

A term used for the number of years an actuary is able to competently perform their duties due to the nature of the work

V

Value dating
When value or credit is given for funds transferred between banks

Alternative meaning
Finding out how much money your dinner date is worth in order to make a relationship decision (used to select the right partner)

Variable
An element in a model

Alternative meaning
Anything than can throw anything off course at anytime (a popular word frequently used by politicians)

Venture capital
An investment in a start up business that is believed to have excellent growth prospects but does not have access to capital markets

Alternative meaning
The name for capital that takes its owners on an adventure journey that is only partly known

Vesting
A guideline stipulating that employees must be entitled to their benefits from a pension fund, profit-sharing plan or employee stock ownership plan, within a certain period of time, even if they no longer work for their employer

Alternative meaning
The act of leaving a high rise building using the parachute vest that is now a legal requirement for all traders working in high rise buildings

W

Waiver of premium
An option in an insurance contract where the payment of premiums are permanently or temporarily stopped if the policyholder is incapacitated

Alternative meaning
The behaviour associated with saying goodbye to top performers within an organisation (to wave at the premium as they leave)

War chest
Cash kept aside for a takeover or for defence against a takeover bid

Alternative meaning
Another name for the money tax payers are required to pay in order to subsidise government bailouts and mistakes (also defence spending)

Warrant
A security entitling the holder to buy a proportionate amount of stock at some specified future date at a specified price

Alternative meaning
An investment that results in the arrest of the investment mangers

Whisper stock
A stock rumoured to be the target of a takeover bid, drawing in speculators who hope to make a profit after the takeover is completed

Alternative meaning
Assets that it is not a good idea to talk about in public

Wholesale
Selling goods in relatively large quantities at prices lower than retail

Alternative meaning
When everything has to go in order to survive (a whole sale)

Windfall profit
A sudden unexpected profit uncontrolled by the profiting party

Alternative meaning
Profit made by insurance companies as a result of premium increases and exclusion clauses on storm damage buildings insurance policies

Working capital
Defined as the difference between current assets and current liabilities and excluding short-term debt

Alternative meaning
The cash required within a company to pay workers for that month

Wrap account
An investment consulting relationship for management of a client's funds by one or more money managers, that bills all fees and commissions in one comprehensive fee charged quarterly

Alternative meaning
The name given for a corporate account with a health food shop

Write down
Reducing the book value of an asset if its is overstated compared to current market values

Alternative meaning
The action it is advisable to take when anyone says anything to do with a business decision

Write off
Charging an asset amount to expense or loss, such as through the use of depreciation and amortisation of assets

Alternative meaning
An investment vehicle you no longer trust (I've gone right off equities)

X

Ex dividend (XD)
The stock is trading with no dividend

Alternative meaning
The money that is agreed and paid to an ex partner or spouse in settlement of a relationship dispute

Y

Yield
The percentage rate of return paid on a stock in the form of dividends, or the effective rate of interest paid on a bond or note

Alternative meaning
To what degree one is prepared to change ones original investment strategy in order to generate profit (OK I yield or give in)

Yield elbow
Point on the yield curve at which the interest rate is the highest

Alternative meaning
Arm wrestling in the office for money and loosing (to yield to someone)

Z

Z Bond
A bond on which interest accrues but is not currently paid to the investor but rather is added to the principal balance of the Z bond and becomes payable upon satisfaction of all prior bond classes

Alternative meaning
A bond whose performance leaves investors feeling sleepy due to its lack of movement

www.ingramcontent.com/pod-product-compliance
Lightning Source LLC
Chambersburg PA
CBHW031325040426
42443CB00005B/213